DEC 1 2 2019

D1256065

DEC 1 2 2019

The BIG Problem
(AND THE SQUIRREL WHO EVENTUALLY SOLVED IT)
Understanding Adjectives and Adverbs

by Nancy Loewen

illustrated by Kevin Sherry

PICTURE WINDOW BOOKS
a capstone imprint

The squirrels had a problem.

A BIG problem.

A scaly, striped, and spotted problem.

A problem with three teeth, tiny horns, and a sturdy tail.

Note: In this story, adjectives are red, and adverbs are green.

The Problem was sitting over the spot
where the squirrels buried their best acorns.

The squirrels huddled together.

"What should we do? What should we do?" they chattered worriedly.

"I have an idea," said the smallest squirrel.

But no one listened.

"Let's watch the Problem for a while," said the oldest squirrel.

So they did.

The Problem slowly scratched its ear.

It lazily picked its nose.

It took a nap and snored ... loudly.

The Problem talked to its mother on the phone.

"Yup, everything is fine, Ma," it said. "But my new neighbors are strange. They twitch their tails a lot. And they're always watching me."

"Now what? Now what?" the squirrels chattered nervously.

"I have an idea," said the smallest squirrel.

But no one listened.

"Let's try to lure it away with food!" said the plumpest squirrel.

So they did.

They gathered berries, seeds, and a pile of second-best acorns.

They arranged the food quite nicely on a leaf. Then they hid in the trees and waited to see what the Problem would do.

9

The Problem sniffed
the air curiously.

But the Problem didn't budge.
Instead it stretched out its sturdy
tail, scooped up the leaf, and ate
the treats in one slurpy swallow.

11

"What next? What next?" the squirrels chattered anxiously.

"I have an idea," said the smallest squirrel.

But no one listened.

"Let's throw things at it!" said the most daring squirrel.

So they did.

They threw twigs, sticks, and branches. They threw pebbles. The most daring squirrel threw a battered old golf ball.

The Problem looked annoyed.
But it still didn't move.

Instead it whispered into *its* phone.

"I don't understand *these* neighbors at all, Ma. First they stare at me. Then they make me a *nice appetizer* plate. And just now they did a *weird* dance, jumping up and down and tossing sticks and things. I'm *baffled*."

The squirrels groaned.

"Well, I guess we've tried everything," said the grumpiest squirrel. "Those acorns are lost to us forever."

"We didn't try
EVERYTHING," said
the smallest squirrel.

And with that, the smallest squirrel approached the Problem and held out his paw.

"Hello," he said. "My name is Skitter. Welcome to the neighborhood."

The Problem blinked once ... twice. Then it held out its paw too.

"I'm Pat," it said. "Very nice to meet you."

Skitter took a deep breath.

"You probably don't know this," he said, "but you're sitting over the spot where we bury our best acorns. Could you please move?"

Pat blinked once ... twice. Then Pat said kindly, "Of course. I'm glad you said something. I had no idea!"

From that moment on, Pat and the squirrels were friends.

GOOD friends.

About Adjectives and Adverbs

Adjectives and adverbs are special words called modifiers.
They add detail and meaning to other words.

Adjectives

Adjectives describe nouns or pronouns, which are words for people, places, or things. Take another look at the opening of the story you just read:

The squirrels had a problem. A BIG problem. A scaly, striped, and spotted problem. A problem with three teeth, tiny horns, and a sturdy tail.

The first sentence doesn't have any modifiers. It has squirrels. It has a problem. And that's it. But the next three phrases tell us a lot. The problem (a noun) is BIG (an adjective). It's also SCALY, STRIPED, and SPOTTED. It has THREE teeth. Its horns are TINY, and its tail is STURDY.

Possessive adjectives modify nouns by showing ownership.

The squirrels twitch their tails. (Which tails did the squirrels twitch? THEIR tails.)

Adverbs

Adverbs are words that describe verbs, but they might also describe adjectives, other adverbs, and even entire phrases. Adverbs answer questions like how, where, when, how often, and to what extent.

Many adverbs end in "ly." Those are the easiest ones to spot.

It lazily picked its nose. (How did the Problem pick its nose? LAZILY.)

But not all adverbs end in "ly." And just because a word ends in "ly" doesn't mean it's an adverb!

I'll call you later. (When will you call? LATER.)

They're always watching me. (How often are the squirrels watching? ALWAYS.)

Could you move a bit? (To what extent should you move? A BIT.)

Now you know a lot about awesome adjectives and amazingly useful adverbs!

Read More

Cleary, Brian P. *Lazily, Crazily, Just a Bit Nasally: More About Adverbs.* Words Are Categorical. Minneapolis: Millbrook Press, 2008.

Ganeri, Anita. *Describing Words: Adjectives, Adverbs, and Prepositions.* Getting to Grips with Grammar. Chicago: Heinemann Library, 2012.

Riggs, Kate. *Adverbs.* Grammar Basics. Mankato, Minn.: Creative Education, 2013.

Internet Sites

FactHound offers a safe, fun way to find Internet sites related to this book. All of the sites on FactHound have been researched by our staff.

Here's all you do:

Visit *www.facthound.com*

Type in this code: 9781479569656

Check out projects, games and lots more at
www.capstonekids.com

Special thanks to our adviser, Terry Flaherty, PhD, Professor of English, Minnesota State University, Mankato, for his expertise.

Editor: Jill Kalz
Designer: Ted Williams
Creative Director: Nathan Gassman
Production Specialist: Katy LaVigne
The illustrations in this book were created digitally.

Picture Window Books are published by Capstone,
1710 Roe Crest Drive, North Mankato, Minnesota 56003
www.capstonepub.com

Copyright © 2016 by Picture Window Books, a Capstone imprint. All rights reserved. No part of this publication may be reproduced in whole or in part, or stored in a retrieval system, or transmitted in any form or by any means, electronic, mechanical, photocopying, recording, or otherwise, without written permission of the publisher.

Library of Congress Cataloging-in-Publication Data
Loewen, Nancy, 1964–
  The BIG Problem (and the squirrel who eventually solved it) : understanding adjectives and adverbs / by Nancy Loewen.
     pages cm.—(Picture window books. Language on the loose.)
  Includes bibliographical references and index.
  Summary: "Introduces adjectives and adverbs as parts of speech through the telling of an original story"—Provided by publisher.
  ISBN 978-1-4795-6965-6 (library binding)
  ISBN 978-1-4795-6969-4 (paperback)
  ISBN 978-1-4795-6973-1 (eBook PDF)
1. English language—Parts of speech—Juvenile literature. 2. English language—Adverb—Juvenile literature. 3. English language—Adjective—Juvenile literature. 4. English language—Parts of speech—Study and teaching (Elementary) I. Title.
PE1199.L64 2016
425'.5—dc23
                                    2014049206

Look for all the books in the series:

The BIG Problem (and the Squirrel Who Eventually Solved It)
Understanding Adjectives and Adverbs

The Duckster Ducklings Go to Mars
Understanding Capitalization

Frog. Frog? Frog!
Understanding Sentence Types

Monsters Can Mosey
Understanding Shades of Meaning

Sasha Sings
Understanding Parts of a Sentence

They're Up to Something in There
Understanding There, Their, and They're

whatever says mark
Knowing and Using Punctuation

When and Why Did the Horse Fly?
Knowing and Using Question Words

Printed in the United States of America in North Mankato, Minnesota.   062015   008823CGF15